How to Make Chocolate at Home, from Bean-to-Bar
A PRACTICAL GUIDE TO FABULOUS CHOCOLATE

Dr Thomas D Avery

Copyright © 2017 D r Thomas D Avery

All rights reserved.

ISBN-13: 978-1984049889

DEDICATION

This book is dedicated to the selfless bean-to-bar chocolate makers that have given freely their knowledge and wisdom. Particularly to John Nanci, the godfather of home-made bean-to-bar chocolate making and founder of Chocolate Alchemy.

The Enjoyment of Chocolate

Excitement

Bliss

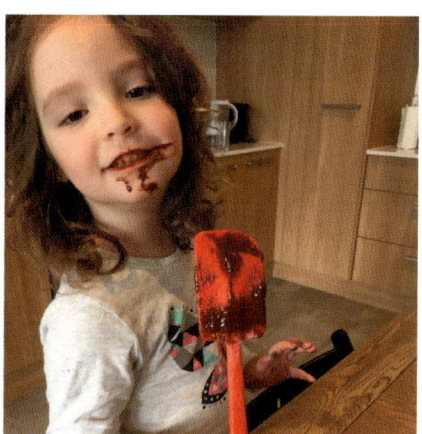
Satisfaction

CONTENTS

	Welcome	i
1	From Beans to Nibs	1
2	Cocoa Liquor	7
3	Adding Sugar	13
4	Adding Cocoa Butter	22
5	Replacing Cocoa Beans	31
6	Cooking with Real Chocolate	43
	Index	53
	About the Author	54
	Acknowledgements	56

WELCOME

The aim of this book is to enable you to make fabulous chocolate the simplest way with minimal specialist equipment in your own home. It will take you from complete novice to expert, with simple to follow instructions, handy tips and extensive formulations for all types of chocolate.

I have over 10 years' experience in making chocolate, bean-to-bar, in my home kitchen. With a day job and two children, I am very time poor, so I have this down to a fine art! I ask you to trust me, try a bunch of things from this book and from there adjust the formulations to your liking and before long you will have your own style. With all the options and information in this book, my aim is to fast track you to your individual chocolate maker style! The important thing is to enjoy the process and really, what is not to like about making fabulous chocolate.

One thing I love about the craft chocolate industry is that everyone is so happy to be working with chocolate. I have had so many wonderful afternoons talking chocolate with like-minded individuals and I invite you to do the same. Get some beans, get involved and reach out to others through the online forums at Chocolate Alchemy by John Nanci and The Chocolate Life by Clay Gordon and other social media platforms, go and visit your local craft chocolate maker and make friends. You won't be disappointed!

Thomas D Avery

FROM BEANS TO NIBS

Cacao beans come from the fruit of *Theobroma cacao* a tropical tree whose botanical name means 'Food of the Gods' which I and many others find somewhat appropriate.

The cacao plant fruits constantly. However, there are two major harvesting times during the year. The pods, which grow directly from the trunk and branches, are cut from the trees and then broken open to retrieve the pulp covered seeds or beans as they are mostly referred to. The mucilage covered seeds are then fermented. This is done in a variety of ways: in piles under banana leaves, in fermentation boxes, in bags or in controlled fermentations in vats. Fermentation can be as short as a couple of days to as long as a week and progresses through alcoholic fermentation driven by yeasts, then malolactic followed by acetobactic fermentations driven by bacteria. Other fungi and molds can also play a role in the fermentation process. The mass of beans can reach temperatures up to 50°C during the acetobacter fermentation step. Fermentation is responsible for killing the bean and producing the chocolate flavor and aroma precursor compounds in the seed. These precursor compounds are essential, so that when you roast your beans, you achieve those amazing reactions that give chocolate its incredible flavor and aroma.

Once fermentation is completed the beans are dried on patios or racks or in drying ovens to remove most of the water, down to about 7%. This gets the beans travel ready.

Receiving and Storing Beans

There are many places now that will sell cacao beans to the home chocolate maker from a couple of kilograms to 10-20 kilograms. I find it is a bit impractical to keep more than 15 kilograms of beans on hand as they have to be stored so that they don't get infected by fungus or parasites. The reality is that the amount that you will probably be able to process in your spare time is limited to several kilograms at once.

The quality and origin of the beans you buy is really going to impact the flavor and quality of the chocolate that you produce. Look carefully at the reviews on the places from which you may source your beans! Cut tests for bean quality determination will be a bit redundant since the beans you buy from retailers selling to small scale bean-to-bar chocolate makers will have likely already done this.

I store my beans by keeping them in large plastic tubs that are NOT airtight, as this will keep them from getting a fungus infection. You will know if your beans have a fungal infection as the shells will be covered in a blue-green powdery fungus and they will smell musty. A low humidity environment is also desirable for the storage of cacao. Good cacao should look like rough almonds and smell rich and acidic due to the residual acetic acid from the final stage of fermentation.

The other issue you need to be aware of when storing beans is weevils. These may be present in the batches you buy or they may get in as you store them. You will be able to see the larvae or moths in your batch of beans if you are unlucky. Some of the suppliers that sell small quantities of beans will be storing their beans using the following method described, which means they will be weevil free and you won't have to carry out any further process. Check with the supplier.

The most effective way to store beans and prevent weevil infestation is to put some dry ice in a small Styrofoam container and place the container in the large tub in which you will be storing your beans. Put your beans into the tub around the dry ice container. Place the lid on your tub and let the dry ice sublime until it is all gone. This will fill the container and surround the beans with an atmosphere of carbon dioxide since carbon dioxide gas is heavier than air. Leave the container undisturbed for two days and then repeat the process. The carbon dioxide atmosphere around your beans will suffocate any moths or larvae that are present in your beans or that hatch during that time. This is a very easy way to control weevils in small amounts of beans without the use of pesticides and without contaminating your beans.

Dry ice expands in volume a lot from a solid to a gas; for example 44g will sublime to fill a volume of 24 liters so you won't need much dry ice to displace the volume of air in your container. In fact 40-50g should do most large containers.

If you are going to use all of your beans straight away you won't need to bother about this step.

Sorting Beans

The beans you receive will likely not be sorted or graded, they will be straight from the farm as a basic agricultural product. You will want to sort through them to remove any metal pieces, stones, sticks and other things before you proceed. Depending on the preparation of the beans you will also want to remove the following types of beans as they will negatively impact the flavor of your chocolate.

Flat Beans

There is very little nib inside these beans so it is best to remove them when you see them.

Very Small Beans

These will become over roasted due to their small size. If you have a great many of these then keep them and you can do a roast profile specifically for these mini-beans.

Bean Clusters

Beans in these clusters are likely to be under fermented or poorly dried. You don't want either of these scenarios as both types will negatively affect your chocolate's flavor. If the beans are only loosely stuck together, just separate them so that they will roast evenly.

Cut Beans

The cut was likely made before the fermentation when the beans were removed from the cacao pod. The inside of the bean is therefore exposed to the fermentation juices and the fermentation doesn't work correctly. These beans look and taste bad.

Broken Beans

Over-roasting of the nib fragments will potentially add a burnt flavor to your chocolate if there are too many of them.

Germinated Beans

These have the germ poking out of the bean and it is a sign that they had germinated before the fermentation process. These beans simply don't taste as good so get rid of them.

It is quite manageable to spread a couple of kilograms of beans out on a table and then sort them quickly, pushing the beans, as you sort them, into a new pile and discarding any of the above types as you go. You can be as thorough as you like with this process. You will get quite quick at this and the quality of your chocolate will thank you for it.

Roasting Beans

This is the most important step, in terms of flavor development, for your finished chocolate. There are now specialist home roasters you can buy but I find that I get amazing results with a conventional oven. The length of time you roast for will depend heavily on the size and origin of the beans you are roasting. Most suppliers will be able to give you a guide on the roasting temperature and time for your beans.

My process for roasting is to place 800g – 1kg of beans in a baking tray with a high wall in a layer no more than two beans thick. You can of course go bigger and do multiple trays depending on the size and efficiency of your oven. I start my oven off at 170°C and warm it up, I then put my tray of beans in and turn the temperature to

150°C. I stir the beans in the tray every 5 minutes. After about the 25 minute mark I will start tasting the beans to see if they are ready. The way I do this is to select two beans of different size, without burning myself, remove the shell and the germ (looks like a nail in the end of the bean) and pop them in my mouth with about a half teaspoon of sugar. I then crunch these together to a paste in my mouth to give me a good approximation of what the finished chocolate will be like. Of course this isn't perfect and certain flavor notes will diminish and others become more pronounced as you turn the beans into chocolate but I find it much easier than just tasting the beans on their own without sugar. Typically a roasting time at 150°C will be between 30 and 50 minutes, you should be able to find your beans sweet spot in their somewhere. This is really where your chocolate making style will come from, this and the formulations that you use for your chocolate.

Once the beans are done, your house will smell amazing! Take the beans out of the oven and you can either let them cool in the tray or transfer them to another tray to cool them down quicker. Once the beans are cooled you can store them in a container for later use or use them straight away.

Cracking and Winnowing

To crack your beans, get a good sturdy fabric bag and dedicate it to this process. Put about half a kilogram of beans in the bag, lay it flat on a solid surface and roll a rolling pin over them to break them. Do not bash them with the rolling pin, you only want to break the shell to separate the nib from the shell. The crushed internal bean fragments are referred to as nibs. The next step of winnowing works best with as large a nibs as possible. Once you have gone over the beans in the bag several times with the rolling pin transfer them to a soil sieve sitting over a large container. Shake the sieve to let the nibs and shell fragments pass through, this keeps back larger pieces and whole beans that didn't get crushed. Generally everything that falls through will be separate nibs and shell. Transfer back anything that didn't go through the sieve and roll again in the bag, then put back in the sieve. You can keep putting through half kilo batches until you are done.

Once all the beans have been crushed and passed through the soil sieve I then run this a through a fine sieve to remove the really fine cocoa dust. Just do this over the garden a couple of handfuls at a time and shake the sieve until no more dust comes through. You can skip this step but I wouldn't recommend it as it makes the step of winnowing very dusty and you will be covered, unless you build yourself a good winnower.

There are lots of plans on the internet for making winnowers and I have made one myself; however, for a couple of kilos of beans at a time I still find that a high walled baking tray and a hair dryer work very well and are quick to set up. Besides, the idea of this book is to do bean-to-bar chocolate as simply as possible without purchasing or building specialist equipment.

To winnow your nibs, put a shallow layer of the nib and shell mix, that has been run through the sieves, in a tray and blow over this with the hair dryer on low with no heat. Move it in a circular motion about 20-30cm above the layer of nib and shell and shake the tray at the same time. Adjust the distance away from the nib and shell mix depending on what you see being blown out of the tray. It won't take long for you to develop a technique where you are just blowing off the lighter shell and leaving the nib in the tray. Once you are done you can always go through by hand and remove any larger heavier pieces of shell; there are always a couple of pieces. I find it best to do winnowing outside with an extension cord on the hair dryer and blow the shell directly into the garden bed.

After winnowing I store my nibs in an air tight container as you would any dry food product. With nibs in hand you are ready for the next step.

Nibs

Getting to the nibs stage of making chocolate is certainly the lion's share of the process. If you want to fast track your chocolate making experience you can purchase nibs from a number of suppliers now and also from grocery stores. Just be aware of what you are getting; are they roasted or raw nibs? If you do get some nibs and they don't tell you whether they are roasted or raw, just taste a small amount with some sugar as I have mentioned above in the roasting section. If they taste like chocolate then they are roasted, if they don't then you will need to roast them. Roasting nibs is simple. Just spread them out on a tray and put them in a preheated oven at 150°C. You will want to start assessing them using the sugar tasting method around the 10 minute mark since nibs are much smaller than beans so their roasting time is shorter.

Once you have nibs you are ready to make chocolate. However, you can also use nibs as nut alternatives in many baked goods, trail mixes or in yogurt or custard. I highly recommend using them as an inclusion in the chocolate you are about to make, they make such an incredible addition.

COCOA LIQUOR

From this point on you will need the only piece of equipment that I would class as specialist equipment, the bench top stone grinder. Make sure that you purchase one that is recommended for chocolate making as the grind times for chocolate extend from a few hours to make cocoa liquor up to 12 to 14 hours to make a single kilogram of finished chocolate. A quality stone grinder is a good investment. I have had my modified Spectra 10 for over 10 years and have used it to make chocolate on average about once every 2 – 3 weeks, which is a great many hours. I have replaced the belt twice and refurbished the motor once and replaced the bearings once, which I think is pretty impressive.

When you receive your grinder there will be some instructions on how to prepare your grinder to start making chocolate. Generally, the process is to grind something like sugar or rice in it for a few hours dry, several times, this will remove the stone dust. Once that is done you can wash your grinder with warm water but make sure that it is completely dry as any water can cause the chocolate you are making to seize. Don't use detergent to wash your grinder; this may taint the grinding stones as they could absorb some of the detergent which will impart a bad flavor to your chocolate.

Making Cocoa Liquor

This chapter concerns the making of cocoa liquor, which is the cocoa nibs, as outlined in the previous chapter, ground to a fine paste. The cocoa liquor can then be used in your chocolate formulations or in cooking. I find using cocoa liquor in my chocolate formulations a better option as there are more liquid components loaded into the grinder. Cocoa liquor is about 50% insoluble material so it is best to grind this as fine as possible to get a beautiful smooth mouth feel for your chocolate. The other 50% that makes up the cocoa liquor is cocoa butter, the fat that gives chocolate its snap and melt-in-the-mouth properties.

Cocoa beans are rather soft so you can achieve an acceptable particle size after only a couple of hours grinding. By acceptable particle size I mean that you can no longer detect a grittiness on your tongue. For those of you that like to be a bit more quantitative this means that the particle sizes are around 15-20 microns. For my particular grinder which has a maximum capacity of 3kg, it takes about 2 hours to grind 500g of cocoa nibs into cocoa liquor. This timeframe is a rough guide as grinders will vary in volume, speed, grinding surface area, grinding surface contact force etc. In contrast to this, the time to grind 1kg of chocolate with sugar and milk powder in it is 12-14 hours with my grinder and that is starting with cocoa liquor.

From a cooking aspect I love and prefer using cocoa liquor for cooking. I find that using cocoa liquor gives you great control over the sweetness of what you are making as well as enabling a chocolate intensity not achievable with finished chocolate. For uses of cocoa liquor in cooking see Chapter 6: Cooking with Real Chocolate.

Your grinder will be noisy; anything that involves two stone surfaces rolling rapidly over each other is going to create a decent noise, so pick where you want your grinder to reside as it will be there making noise for a good few hours or days. I run mine in the laundry with the door shut or in the garage.

Starting the Grind

Firstly, I take my nibs and put them in a food processor and blitz them to get a fine and even particle size. Don't blitz them for too long as it will wear out your food processor and start to turn the nibs to a paste making them difficult to transfer. This step is just to get rid of the bigger nibs so that the rollers of the grinder don't have any troubles and get stuck.

Irrespective of the ambient temperature I always warm my grinder and nibs before-hand. To do this I heat my oven to 100°C for about 10 minutes, turn it off and put the grinder bowl and stone rollers into the oven with a ceramic bowl containing the blitzed nibs. After 10 minutes in the oven the grinder and nibs will be nice and warm. Assemble the grinder and add about 100g of nib and turn the grinder on, keep adding 100g portions to the grinder every few minutes. Keep the lid on the grinder for this process as bits of nib paste will flick out all over the place. The grinder will reduce the nibs to a free flowing paste in short order, after this it is a case of grinding for long enough to reduce the particle size. If the temperature in the room where you are grinding is low sometimes the grinder will cool down and the paste will thicken and solidify. This is bad for your grinder as it will wear out your grinder's motor or the belt running the bowl. If this starts to happen use a hair dryer to warm the bowl until the paste becomes free flowing again. In general though, with the pre-heating step the heat from the friction of the grinding wheels against the stone base of the grinder will be enough to keep the liquor warm and fluid.

I find with my grinder that the evenness of the grind benefits from periodically scraping down the sides of the grinder and scraping the edges of the grinding stones as some areas in the grinder just don't mix as evenly. You will be able to identify areas in your grinder that don't mix well as you will see a build-up of granular nibs; just periodically scrape these areas with a spatula during the grind.

To know when your cocoa liquor is to an acceptable fineness without using a micrometer, just taking a small amount, put it on your tongue and rubbing it against the roof of your mouth. If it is rough you will need to grind for longer. A more palatable way of testing the liquor is by taking some of the liquor and making it into a hot chocolate, a recipe for which can be found in the Cooking with Real Chocolate chapter. If you find a gritty residue at the bottom of your hot chocolate then you need to grind for longer.

Conching

Conching is the process of heating and manipulating the chocolate in order to drive off some of the volatile acids and to increase the fat coating and smooth off the edges of the particles in the chocolate. This process changes the flavor of the chocolate and improves the mouthfeel of the chocolate. With a bench top stone grinder, conching is achieved by removing the lid of the grinder for some of the grind to let the volatile compounds escape and by increasing the grind time to improve the fat coating of particles. For producing cocoa liquor you will not need to conch unless you are planning to eat the cocoa liquor as a 100% chocolate. Generally, though 100% chocolate is made using cocoa liquor and added cocoa butter to reduce its intensity. I have not met many people that eat cocoa liquor straight up.

Emptying and Cleaning the Grinder

Once your grind is completed you will need to pour out the cocoa liquor. Some grinders have a tipping mechanism, some you will need to remove the stone rollers, scrape them off and then scrape the bowl out. You will never get all the liquor or chocolate out of your grinder. If you are interested to know how much is typically left in your grinder just weigh the cocoa liquor and compare that value to the amount of nibs that you originally put into the grinder. For my grinder this is typically 40-50g; this can be important if you don't plan to wash out your grinder between each grind. I rarely wash out my grinder unless I am doing something specific like switching from dark chocolate to white chocolate. Sometimes I will adjust my formulation to take into account this residue, sometimes I don't, it really depends on the impact you think it will have on the next batch of chocolate.

If you do decide to wash your grinder, just take the parts apart, wash them with a stiff brush in hot water and allow them to dry thoroughly. You will probably need to push tissue paper through the holes in various parts of the grinder as whatever you are grinding has a way of getting into every nook and cranny.

Making Cocoa Butter and Depleted Cocoa Liquor

Why would you want to make your own cocoa butter from your beans? There are several reasons:

- cocoa butter is expensive
- the beans used for cocoa butter production aren't usually the most fabulous
- many suppliers don't stipulate the origin of the cocoa butter
- if you make your own cocoa butter from your own beans and use it to make chocolate you can claim 100% single origin status because all of the cocoa solids (cocoa liquor + cocoa butter) come from the same origin.

Cocoa liquor is for all intents and purposes made up of 50% cocoa butter and 50% insoluble material. This 50:50 split is an approximation; the fat content of cocoa beans can vary from about 45% up to 60% and depends on the variety and the location in which it is grown.

Some of the cocoa butter is easily separated from the cocoa liquor by taking your finely ground cocoa liquor and keeping it warm and liquid for up to 7 days. During this time the insoluble solids will settle to the bottom and the fat (cocoa butter) will rise to the surface and form a layer on the top. It is then a matter of removing the cocoa butter from the remaining cocoa liquor which is done by allowing the cocoa butter and cocoa liquor to set solid and you can then just chip the cocoa butter off the top of the cocoa liquor.

This technique works best if you have more than 2.5kg of cocoa liquor as it is easier to keep this amount liquid for several days. The method I use to keep liquor liquid for days is to pour it into my slow cooker pot and periodically turn it on to warm for 10-15 minutes, then turn it off and then back on when it cools down. This will keep the liquor at around 40-60°C. Alternatively, if the weather is fine and warm I just put the slow cooker outside in the sun, which heats it up and keeps the liquor liquid. If you do put it in the sun, make sure the cocoa liquor is protected from direct sunlight. If the lid of your slow cooker is glass then cover it with foil as the sunlight can cause undesirable reactions to occur leading to some funky flavors and aromas that you don't want in your chocolate or cocoa butter.

The amount of cocoa butter you will be able to recover will depend on the fat content of your cocoa beans. If you are lucky and have beans with a high fat content you might get up towards 10% cocoa butter recovered which is about 250g from 2.5kg of cocoa liquor. This will be enough to make a few kilos of chocolate as outlined in the following chapters. If your beans have a low fat content then you might only get around 5% cocoa butter, which is still enough to experiment with.

The cocoa liquor left over, which has had some of the cocoa butter removed, I refer to as 'depleted cocoa liquor'. This depleted cocoa liquor can be used to make hot chocolates as you would with cocoa liquor or you can use it in Chapter 3: Adding Sugar, to make eating chocolate and chocolate spreads which don't require the addition of cocoa butter.

Tempering

Unless you are planning to mold the cocoa liquor into bars and eat it you do not need to temper and mold it, just store it as it sets until you either use it to make chocolate or for cooking. If you want to temper it see the tempering instructions in the next chapter.

Flavoring Cocoa Liquor

Why would you want to flavor cocoa liquor? Well to cook with it and to make the best hot chocolates you will ever have! Chapter 6: Cooking with Real Chocolate contains a host of recipes using cocoa liquor.

There are two ways to flavor your cocoa liquor, you can use an oil based flavoring such as orange oil or mint oil, or you can grind the flavoring in as you grind the nibs into liquor.

For flavoring oils use about 8-9 drops of the oil in 500g of cocoa liquor. This can be done after the grind so as not to drive off the flavor during the grinding.

For spices and other things like coffee you will need to grind them with the nibs into a liquor. I love hot chocolates and flavored hot chocolates are a passion of mine so I have included a list of what I think are fabulously flavored liquors.

Mocha

Chocolate beautifully enhanced with a touch of real coffee, just grind 5% coffee beans by weight into cocoa liquor.

Mint Mocha

Mint, coffee and chocolate a strange and beautiful thing. Take the mocha liquor made above and add 8-9 drops of mint oil for every 500g of mocha liquor.

Cinnamon

After several hundred years of evolution at Spanish hands and palates this recipe from 1701 allows us to create a perfectly balanced drink. Grind one third of a vanilla bean and 1g of cinnamon into 600g of cocoa liquor.

Cinnamon Mocha

I think cinnamon and coffee go well together and adding them both to chocolate is amazing. Grind 1g of cinnamon, 8 mm of vanilla bean and 25g of freshly roasted coffee beans into 500g of cocoa liquor.

Creole

A traditional drink of Trinidad, a place rich in chocolate history, this drink is flavored with nutmeg, cinnamon and bay leaf. Grind 1g of cinnamon, 1 bay leaf (dried) and 1g of nutmeg into 600g of cocoa liquor.

Gingerbread

This hot chocolate takes me back to my childhood. Grind 2g of dried ginger, 1g of nutmeg, 1g of cinnamon and 0.5g of cloves into 600g of cocoa liquor.

Liquorice Bullet

Bite…..no drink the bullet! Grind 0.5g of star anise, 0.5g of liquorice root into 600g of cocoa liquor.

Cardamom

The 'Food of the Gods' and the 'Queen of Spices', a perfect and fragrant match, I really love this! Grind 1g of cardamom pods into 600g of cocoa liquor

Jasmine

Cacao perfumed with jasmine is something I came across in Sophie D. and Michael D. Coe's book 'The True History of Chocolate'. The story goes that renowned scientist Francesco Redi was the inventor and jealous protector of the recipe for jasmine scented hot chocolate, the favorite drink of the Grand Duke of Tuscany, Cosimo III de' Medici. The secret method for its preparation only came to light after Redi's death. The method of production was to infuse cocoa nibs

with jasmine flowers by layering them in a wooden box, each day adding more flowers for almost two weeks. The cacao nib and dried flower mixture was then ground on a metate with cinnamon, ambergris, vanilla and sugar, but not at too high a temperature as excessive heat could drive off the precious scent. The extravagant mixture was then used to make hot chocolate fit for any ruler. This intrigued me; such a secret must mean that this drink is stunning, so I embarked upon some experimental archaeology. Firstly, I needed the right kind of jasmine. My only clue to this was that it was the same jasmine used to flavor green tea. It turns out I required *Jasminium Sambac*, or as the label attached to the plant said when I found it in a local nursery, 'Grand Duke of Tuscany'. The Duke must have loved this plant. At least I knew that I was buying the right one! I was told when purchasing the plant that it was a slow growing vine with a beautiful double flower and amazing scent and that it wasn't as popular as other 'jasmines' due to its slow growth. The plant was just flowering when I bought it and the flowers were unbelievably potent. I found the fragrance much nicer than other 'jasmines'; it is exquisite. I had to wait all winter for the plant to establish and flower again to do my experiment. Now, I like to think of myself as 'just lazy enough', this means that if something looks like it is hard work I try to optimize it. This worked in my favor in this case; instead of layering nibs and flowers and then grinding, I took finely ground or grated cocoa liquor and put it in an air tight glass jar with the flowers inside a calico bag.

After experimenting for a bit I found that you only need 1 jasmine flower to scent 25g of cocoa liquor, only 40 flowers per kilogram, not a lot. Note here that extreme hot weather (over 35°C) will reduce the flower's potency and more may be required. The flowers can be added a few at a time over the course of a week or two as the scent stays with the cocoa liquor in a sealed jar. You can't do this in plastic containers or plastic bags as the scent is lost after a while. The flowers must be removed after about 2 days because as they dry they lose their scent to the cocoa but also start to produce a very herbaceous scent which I felt tainted the cocoa liquor. You will know when to remove each flower as they will start to oxidize and go a purple brown color. Once scented, the cocoa liquor will maintain the scent almost indefinitely if stored in a glass airtight jar, so you can make it during the summer and use it during the winter…..assuming you have such patience.

Well what was it like? Since I am waxing lyrical about it, it must have been fantastic, right? Well yes, it is truly amazing as a hot chocolate, no need to include the cinnamon, ambergris and vanilla. The jasmine scent is just that, a scent, very ethereal and not really a flavor but an aroma that is just sublime. You can use the jasmine flowers to scent other things such as macarons or black tea, just store them in an air tight glass jar with the flowers for a day or more.

Using the jasmine scented cocoa liquor in cooking or to make eating chocolate doesn't really work as both of these processes involve extended periods of heating and this simply drives off the volatile aroma of the jasmine.

ADDING SUGAR

The act of adding sugar will now make your cocoa liquor into what we are used to describing as chocolate. Venturing into this next section you have two ingredients that you can use, cocoa liquor and depleted cocoa liquor, the by-product from the production of cocoa butter. The addition of cocoa butter into chocolate will be covered in the next chapter as we get into more commercial style chocolate formulations. There are two reasons for this; firstly cocoa butter is expensive and secondly the method described in the previous chapter only makes a small amount of cocoa butter in comparison to the depleted cocoa liquor. You will also want to have uses for your depleted cocoa liquor since there is no point in removing the cocoa butter only to add it back.

Chocolate is defined by that snap and mouthfeel where the chocolate melts at body temperature and is solid and shiny at room temperature. It is therefore critical to consider the amount and type of fats in your chocolate formulation. Without the addition of cocoa butter we are limited as to how much of a fat containing ingredient we can add, like nuts and milk powder. If too much in the way of alternative fats are in the formulation it just will not temper very well and will not have that snap that we expect from chocolate.

Water and Chocolate

A note of caution is warranted at this point: water is bad for chocolate, so any ingredient containing water is bad for chocolate. Any water will cause the chocolate you are making to seize which means it will take on a granular texture and become very thick and the fat will start to separate out. For this reason you cannot use ingredients like milk, butter or maple syrup to make chocolate unless they have had the water removed. For the examples I just listed, milk powder, clarified butter or ghee and maple sugar are the water free versions of those ingredients that can be used in chocolate making.

% Chocolate

Before we get into formulating chocolate it is worth explaining the meaning behind the '% chocolate' that you see on chocolate bar packaging. % chocolate just means the total percent of ingredients derived from the cocoa bean, so for fine chocolate this refers to cocoa butter and cocoa liquor. For inferior chocolate this can also include cocoa powder. An example is a 75% dark chocolate could be made up of 70% cocoa liquor and 5% cocoa butter or 65% cocoa liquor and 10% cocoa butter. The % chocolate is used typically as a quality measure showing how much of the expensive cocoa butter and cocoa beans have been used to produce the chocolate. It will also give you an idea of the intensity of the chocolate although this can be misleading if a lot of cocoa butter has been used in the formulation.

100% Single Origin Chocolate

Unless you are one of the unique people that can eat cocoa liquor straight up then you will be wanting to grind sugar into your cocoa liquor to make a chocolate. This chapter is concerned with formulations that do not include the addition of extra cocoa butter. This type of chocolate may be attractive to people for a number of reasons: firstly cocoa butter is reasonably expensive and secondly if it is not produced from the same beans that you are making your chocolate from then your chocolate bar will not be 100% single origin. It is possible to make your own cocoa butter as you would have seen in the previous chapter but it uses a lot of beans as you only get about 5-10%. Besides that, it is possible to make fabulous chocolate without the need to add cocoa butter to the formulation. These chocolates can be a little thicker to work with and they are more intense, toward the darker side but nonetheless they are fabulous! These richly flavored chocolates are my personal preference when I make something for myself.

Types of Sugar

There is quite the choice in the type of sugar you can use to make your chocolate. Some of the more amorphous sugars such as coconut blossom sugar or maple sugar tend not to refine as well but still give an acceptable result. Different sugars can be used to introduce additional flavor notes to the chocolate. For example I use coconut blossom sugar to add a caramel note to chocolate, which, with some salt in the formulation gives a salted caramel flavor to the chocolate.

I have found no advantage in using powdered sugar over granulated sugar of varying sizes, in fact I suspect that the powdered sugar actually increases the grind time, though I have not quantitatively evaluated this.

Types of Milk Powder

As with sugar there is increasing access to interesting milk powders, aside from the full cream and skim cow's milk powders, there are goat and buffalo milk powders, which add very distinct flavors to chocolate. Skim cow's milk powder can be very useful in adjusting the fat percentage in your chocolate so it doesn't get too high; this can be an issue when formulating for white nut chocolates and carob chocolate as you will see it used in Chapter 5: Replacing Cocoa Beans. There is also easier access to caramelized milk powders as well, which will add a totally different dimension to your chocolate.

Vegetable milk powders like coconut or soy can also be used in chocolate for flavor or to create a 'milk' chocolate to accommodate dietary requirements.

Nuts

Nuts are a great way to add in flavor notes to your chocolate and also to reduce the intensity of the chocolate. I recommend freshly roasting your nuts before using in chocolate making so as to maximize their flavor in the chocolate.

Most common nuts have a similar fat percentage to cocoa beans which is around 50%; however some have very high fat contents and this needs to be accounted for when formulating. I have included a table with the percentage fat in common nuts.

Nut	% fat
Peanut	49
Hazelnut	61
Almond	49
Macadamia nut	76
Cashew nut	44
Walnut	65
Pistachio nut	45
Pecan nut	72

Malt Powder

I don't tend to use malt powder in my chocolates. If you want to use it be aware that it is very hydroscopic so you will need to store it in a well-sealed packet or container, especially if you live in a humid environment. If you want to use it in formulations simply treat it as a sugar and replace some of the sugar, typically 5-10%, with malt powder. Malt powders are easily obtained from brewing outlets, as it is used extensively in making beer. Malt is used a lot in making milk chocolates. This is my least favorite type of chocolate and adding malt just makes it taste like Maltesers so I just don't bother. Some chocolate makers use it in dark chocolate formulations where it is specifically paired with a bean of a particular origin. If you like malt, don't be scared to explore.

Other Fats and Oils

We are not adding cocoa butter here in these formulations and I don't really use other fats and oils in chocolate bars but they are useful for making chocolate spreads.

I don't tend to use clarified butter or ghee but they can be used in white chocolate or milk chocolate formulations for flavor and texture.

Essentially flavorless vegetable oils like canola, sunflower or deodorized coconut oil are useful in creating chocolate spreads where you want to keep the chocolate fluid and spreadable at room temperature. Strongly flavored oils such as olive oil or coconut oil can be used for the same purposes but need careful consideration because of the strong flavor.

Salt

Salt can be an interesting addition to chocolate whether ground in or as a crunchy inclusion. I typically use salt ground into a formulation when I am using nuts as it enhances the nuttiness and brings it out in the chocolate. I also use it when I use a caramelized sugar like coconut blossom sugar; the salt gives a salty caramel flavor to the chocolate. Salt as an inclusion will enhance the perceived sweetness of the chocolate on your palate and using a good quality salt or smoked salt can go very nicely with some origins.

Vanilla

Vanilla is a great complement to the flavor of chocolate but it is not necessary to make fabulous chocolate. The amounts of vanilla I recommend in the following formulations are sparing and designed to complement and not dominate the chocolate. If you are a big fan of vanilla and you want to add a lot to your chocolate, go right ahead, make it how you like it. Vanilla bean pieces are also a great addition to stir through chocolate as they give an intense sour/salty vanilla burst.

Raw Chocolate

If you want to make raw chocolate, you have to consider firstly if the fermentation process that the beans go through meets your raw food requirements. As I have mentioned previously the temperature of a cacao bean fermentation reaches 50°C and therefore may not meet the requirement to be classified as a raw food. If this temperature is okay then you just skip the roasting step and move straight to the cracking and winnowing stage of the chocolate making process. Cracking and winnowing unroasted cacao beans has its own issues since the roasting process separates the interior of the bean from the shell. You will probably find that there will be a lot more shell stuck to nibs when cracking and winnowing the unroasted beans. Once you have your unroasted nibs you can use the formulations in the book to make raw chocolate.

Some words of caution here: if you don't roast your cacao beans you will not develop any of the flavor and aroma compounds that give chocolate its distinctive and mouthwatering aroma. Any chocolate you make with raw nibs will not taste like chocolate. You will also run the risk of food poisoning since the roasting process kills the bacteria, yeasts and fungus that may be present from the fermentation process. Remember that a lot of the beans you get will be a basic agricultural product from a third world country. For me, I eat chocolate because of its divine flavor and aroma, not for any health benefits that it may give me, raw or otherwise.

Adding Ingredients to the Grinder

I find the resulting chocolate from a grind is less powdery on the palate if the nibs are ground into liquor before the sugar and other ingredients are added. This is because the nibs contain the insoluble parts of the chocolate and so is best ground as fine as possible. Sugar crystals are very hard and take a lot longer to refine than the nibs; however they are also soluble in your saliva so it doesn't matter too much if they are not super fine.

Warm your grinder as described in the previous chapter and load it with the dry ingredients. Pour in the melted cocoa liquor and start your grind. For chocolate of this type it takes 12-14 hours to grind 1kg of chocolate in my grinder, to an acceptable fineness.

Conching

I don't advocate conching with cocoa liquor as I don't typically eat cocoa liquor. I use it in cooking and I find that the cooking process acts in a similar way to the conching process by driving off some of the volatiles. However, with eating chocolate you will probably want to do some level of conching. Now, it pays not to think of conching as something separate to the grinding process, especially with your home set up, since your grinder is your conch. You can conch at any stage during the grind, this just means taking the lid off of the grinder while it is running. The grinder in a house at an ambient temperature around 23°C will get pretty hot so removing the lid will allow a lot of the volatiles from the chocolate to be released into the air. You will be able to smell the difference. In terms of how long to conch for, keep tasting the chocolate as you grind and conch to see how the flavor is developing. Typically for my grinder, I find that I only ever need a couple of hours of conching with the lid off. If you leave the lid off too long you can over conch your chocolate by driving too many of those lovely volatile flavor and aroma compounds out and your chocolate will taste bland and flat.

Dark Chocolate

This is a common formulation used by craft chocolate makers. I find this formulation is an excellent vehicle to show off the single origin character of a chocolate.

75% cocoa liquor
25% sugar

This is all you need, your other option here is to add vanilla or another spice like cardamom or coffee. I recommend about 8mm of vanilla bean per kg of chocolate, I have found this amount gives just enough to complement the chocolate but not dominate. If you really like vanilla go ahead and add more. For cardamom I recommend 1.5g per kg of chocolate which again is at a level where it complements but doesn't dominate the chocolate. I love a little coffee in this formulation and adding 1% of great freshly roasted coffee beans will give you a fabulous mocha bar.

I also like to use coconut blossom sugar in this formulation with sea salt sprinkled on the back of the finished bar to give a salted caramel chocolate flavor.

Dark Milk Chocolate

Animal Milk Chocolate

70% cocoa liquor
20% sugar
10% full cream milk powder
8mm vanilla bean / kg of chocolate (optional)

This is one of my favorite formulations, I love just a little milk in a dark chocolate to give it a creaminess and take the edge off of the astringency. This formula works with this quite low amount of sugar as milk powder is really quite sweet, with cow's milk powder typically containing around 36% of the sugar lactose.

Coconut Milk Chocolate

65% cocoa liquor
25% sugar

10% coconut milk powder
8mm vanilla bean / kg of chocolate (optional)

This chocolate has a lovely coconut flavor in balance with the cocoa flavor from the chocolate. I find this chocolate works really well with inclusions; my favorite being preserved ginger. The reason the formulation changes here is that coconut milk powder contains about twice as much fat as full cream cow's milk powder but has much less sugar.

Dark Nut Chocolate

65% cocoa liquor
25% sugar
10% nuts finely chopped
0.5g sea salt / kg of chocolate
8mm vanilla bean / kg of chocolate (optional)

Peanuts and hazelnuts are the best here as they have a strong distinct flavor which is required in this formulation in order for the flavor to come through. The amount of nuts cannot really be increased in this setting without the addition of cocoa butter which is covered in the next section. Other nuts will work but they are not present in a high enough amount to compete with the strength of the chocolate flavor. Using 10% of the chosen nut chopped as an inclusion in the finished chocolate will further enhance the nut flavor. This is also the purpose of the addition of sea salt to the formulation, salt enhances the 'nuttiness' flavor of the nut and brings it to the fore. This will be quite a soft chocolate when tempered.

Using Depleted Cocoa Liquor

The process of making the cocoa butter described in the previous chapter results in a depleted cocoa liquor which can be used to make amazing hot chocolates. You can also use it to make chocolate bars as well as chocolate spreads which are excellent. Since there is less cocoa butter in the depleted liquor you can get away with doing a 75% chocolate with the addition of 25% sugar. You can also do higher percentage chocolates, just not much lower than 75%. The use of this depleted cocoa liquor will give a more intense 75% chocolate which I find really nice.

75% depleted cocoa liquor
25% sugar
8 mm vanilla bean/ kg of chocolate (optional)

Inclusions

There are two ways to add 'inclusions' to your chocolate bars, you can either sprinkle them on the back of the bar directly after you have molded the bar or stir the inclusions into the tempered chocolate and then mold the bars. To put the inclusions on the back of the bar, I have no recommendation as to how much, just sprinkle or place things on the bar while the chocolate is still fluid, until you are happy with how it looks, then tap the molds to make sure the inclusions are stuck in the chocolate.

As a general rule for stirring inclusions into the chocolate I stick with 10% by weight of a 'chunk' inclusion, for example 100g of nibs in 1kg of chocolate. I use this rule for chopped nuts, nibs and dried or glace fruit as this amount doesn't make the chocolate too thick for molding and doesn't over power the chocolate.

Cocoa nibs are my favorite inclusion, making any chocolate almost impossible to stop eating, perhaps only topped by caramelized nibs. Glace ginger is also a favorite of mine to pair with the coconut milk chocolate. Let your imagination run wild with dried blueberries, croutons, cereals, ……. anything really.

For inclusions with intense flavors you will need to back off the amount, from the 10% rule of thumb. For vanilla bean pieces, 1 vanilla bean diced finely is enough for 1kg of chocolate. For coffee bean shards I find about 5% by weight is good for me.

For lighter things like freeze dried fruit or crushed honeycomb use about 10-12g in every 500g of chocolate. Both honeycomb and freeze dried fruits are extremely hydroscopic and are best used as internal inclusions as the surrounding chocolate will protect the inclusions from moisture and they will maintain their crunch.

If you want to work with spices as an inclusion or shredded coconut the following amounts and pairings work really well.

Fennel and Salt

Add 17g of fennel seed that has been roughly blitzed in a spice grinder or coffee grinder to 1kg of tempered chocolate and stir through before molding. Sprinkle sea salt on the back of the bar before it has set.

Coriander and Coconut

Add 17g of coriander seed that has been roughly blitzed and 17g of shredded coconut that has also been roughly blitzed to 1kg of tempered chocolate and stir through before molding.

Tempering Chocolate

There are many methods to temper chocolate, this is a quick and low mess method that I use every time for the kitchen scale tempering of 0.5-3kg batches. All you need to do is to melt the chocolate in a heavy glass bowl in the microwave, now don't be scared, just do it in 20 second bursts and once it starts to melt move to 10 second bursts….no dramas, don't forget to stir well between bursts. Now make sure the chocolate is completely melted and has reached a temperature of 40°C or higher, but not too high. This is important, so use a thermometer if you will and for goodness' sake don't burn chocolate. Now let the chocolate cool, stirring every now and then. I use the fridge for this if it is a hot day. Stir every 5-10 minutes, scraping down the sides and along the bottom of the bowl with a spatula. Once the chocolate starts to thicken let it cool out of the fridge a little further with regular stirring and scraping. Leave the spatula in the chocolate as you go through this process. Once the chocolate is about the consistency of toothpaste it is ready for the next step. Put the bowl in the microwave again and microwave in 5 second bursts until the chocolate is back to a nice flowing liquid but don't get it too hot again or you will kill the temper. As a rough guide a 1kg batch of chocolate takes about 20-25 seconds to go from toothpaste stage to ready to mold, depending on the power of your microwave of course. Now your chocolate is in temper and ready to mold, drizzle or spread. Don't believe it is that easy? Well it is, give it a try, you won't ruin the chocolate, the worst that can happen is that you will have to start back at the beginning.

5 Easy Steps

1. Heat chocolate in the microwave until melted and above 40°C.
2. Cool on the bench or in fridge with regular stirring until it just begins to thicken.
3. Cool out of the fridge with regular stirring until toothpaste consistency.
4. Heat back up until just nicely fluid again, not too hot!
5. Mold your chocolate.

If you want to temper your chocolate straight out of the grinder, that is fine, just skip the first step since the grinder temperature will be above 40°C if you have been grinding in it all day.

Molds, Molding and Coating

I whole-heartedly recommend investing in some polycarbonate molds as these will give your bars a very professional finish; however these are what I would call specialist equipment and they are certainly not necessary to start your chocolate making journey. You will need some sort of mold to set your tempered chocolate in and the cheap plastic molds that you can find everywhere will do the job nicely.

When you go to mold your tempered chocolate, you will want to work reasonably quickly, especially if the ambient temperature is cool as the chocolate will set quickly. The way I do it is to place the mold on a set of scales and using a large spoon fill the mold to the desired weight. This will ensure your bars are the same weight and thickness. You don't have to do this of course, you can just eyeball it. Tap, bang and shimmy your mold to get the chocolate level and filling the mold, this also brings bubbles to the surface. Keep this up until no more bubbles rise and pop on the surface.

If you are filling small molds like frogs, hearts or festival molds you might want to use a disposable syringe or piping bag. This will give you pretty good control when filling these little intricate molds.

Once the mold is filled and the bubbles removed I put them in the fridge for a good 5-10 minutes. This will set them quickly and make sure they contract well and release from the mold. You will be able to tell if the chocolate has released by lifting the mold up and looking from underneath where you will be able to see whether the chocolate has pulled away from the plastic.

Once set you can turn the chocolate out of the mold. I usually do this on a board or some plastic wrap on the benchtop so as not to contaminate the bars. Then just wrap in foil or place in a cellophane bag to store. If you are sprinkling freeze dried fruit or crushed honeycomb on the back of a bar as is trendy you will need to keep your bars well sealed away from the air as these things will absorb moisture from the air and become soggy.

Chocolate Spreads

Chocolate nut spreads are amazing when made with your own cocoa liquor. I have formulated this to get both the chocolate and hazelnut flavors in balance and intense.

Cocoa liquor recipe

33% cocoa liquor
19.8% raw sugar
25.5% roasted hazelnuts or peanuts
11.3% canola oil
10.4% full cream milk powder
0.5g sea salt / 1.2 kg of chocolate spread
8 mm vanilla bean/ kg of chocolate (optional)

Once you pour this into jars, stir it now and then as it is cooling and it will thicken as a smooth paste. If you live in a hot climate, use the fridge, just leaving the chocolate spread to cool undisturbed can sometimes lead to the fats crystalizing in a granular form which will make the paste grainy. If this happens just microwave the jar without the lid until the fat crystals melt and try again. This recipe should give a chocolate paste that is nicely spreadable at room temperature.

Hazelnuts can be replaced with other nuts in this recipe as it is reasonably forgiving. It is great with peanuts!

Depleted cocoa liquor recipe

Depleted cocoa liquor is even better for making chocolate nut spreads since the amount of cocoa butter in the formulation is reduced. It is the cocoa butter that can lead to the granular crystallization issue in the above recipe. What better way to reward yourself for harvesting cocoa butter than to make some chocolate spread with the depleted cocoa liquor!

Inclusions

For something exciting try adding inclusions to the chocolate spread. We have chunky peanut butter so why not chunky chocolate spreads. Try adding nibs, chopped nuts or dried fruits, about 10% by weight (100g per kg of spread) should be fine to still maintain a spreadable paste.

ADDING COCOA BUTTER

I have covered making cocoa butter in Chapter 2: Cocoa Liquor, if you are not doing this you will need to purchase your own cocoa butter. Cocoa butter comes either bleached and deodorized or natural; natural cocoa butter still has the aroma compounds so it will potentially add extra chocolate flavor notes to your chocolate. Natural cocoa butter may also have some color to it too.

Commercial Style Chocolate

Cocoa butter is added for several reasons: firstly to create a crisp tempered chocolate, secondly to reduce the intensity of the chocolate, thirdly to create a smooth mouthfeel and finally to improve the fluidity of the chocolate for applications such as dipping. Coverture is the name given to chocolate that has a relatively high percentage of added cocoa butter and is used for coating things. I will not cover any coverture formulations here, though you can convert any of the finished chocolates here to a coverture by simply adding 5-10% extra cocoa butter by weight after you have finished making the chocolate. Since cocoa butter requires no grinding you can just melt it in with your chocolate and then temper and use it.

Lethicin

Lethicin is a controversial ingredient which is used to improve the rheology of the chocolate, which is to say it makes it flow better in a similar way to adding more cocoa butter. Rheology becomes important if you are using machinery to temper and mold your chocolate, which we are not and you will have no trouble hand tempering and molding any of the chocolate formulations in this book. If you are intending to use your chocolate for coating applications, adding lethicin will improve the flow of your chocolate without adding extra cocoa butter which is more expensive.

Lethicin also acts as an emulsifier which is useful if you are planning to use your chocolate in cooking applications, particularly where there is a danger of the mixture separating such as in making a ganache, a chocolate pastry or cookie dough. This also applies to using cocoa liquor for cooking which is covered in the last chapter of this book. The recipes in this book for cooking with chocolate are formulated so the risk of mixtures separating is minimal and I have mentioned tips to avoid separating as well. However, if you would like to use lethicin in your chocolate for coating or in the production of your cocoa liquor for cooking simply add 0.5% lethicin (5g for every kg of chocolate or cocoa liquor) to the mixture at the start and grind it in.

Deconstructing Commercial Chocolate

At some point in your chocolate making journey you will come across a commercial chocolate where you think 'Oh, this is lovely, I wonder how it is formulated as I would like to try to make this'. Well wonder no longer as I have put some equations together to help you deconstruct the formulation of just about any chocolate worth copying.

A lot of commercial chocolate formulations you wouldn't want to copy as they balance the cost of ingredients with a minimally acceptable quality product. I assume though that since you are into chocolate making the quality of the chocolate you are consuming is higher than the average person.

If you are handy with computers it is simple to program a spreadsheet with these formulas to make it very easy to determine the composition of a commercial chocolate formulation.

One thing that can throw the calculations out is if cocoa powder is listed as an ingredient. This is because it is hard to know the fat content of the powder used because it can vary considerably. However, if they are using this as an ingredient it is usually to standardize the flavor profile for mass production and you probably don't want to copy that formulation anyway.

Disclaimer: There is potential for there to be some error or approximation in the information on packaging and the estimations I make for percentages of fat and sugars in cocoa liquor and milk powder. Your results from these equations to deconstruct the chocolate formulations will depend on the accuracy of this information. The dark chocolate calculator will be more accurate than the milk chocolate calculator simply because there are less inputs and estimates, thus reducing the chances of error. That said I have found these equations to work quite well.

Formulation calculators assume the following:

1. Dark chocolate is composed of sugar, cocoa liquor/mass/beans and cocoa butter. This calculation doesn't take into account the small amounts of lecithin or vanilla added to certain chocolates.
2. Milk chocolate is composed of sugar, cocoa liquor/mass/beans, cocoa butter and full cream/whole milk powder. This calculation doesn't take into account the small amount of lecithin or vanilla added to certain chocolates.
3. The calculator doesn't work if cocoa powder, cream powder, skim milk powder, coffee, nuts, clarified butter, ghee or anything else that isn't stipulated above, has been used as an ingredient in the chocolate.
4. That cocoa liquor (which is just crushed cocoa beans) has a 50% fat content.
5. That percent cocoa solids is cocoa liquor/mass/beans + cocoa butter.
6. That full cream milk powder contains 26% fat and 36% lactose (type of sugar).

Don't be put off by the math, I have taken care of all of the complex equation solving. All you need to do is start from the top and add in the known values from the chocolate package and solve for each ingredient. I have included a worked example for each calculator.

Dark Chocolate Calculator

You will need two pieces of information from your favorite chocolates packaging, the percent cocoa solids which is usually proudly stated on the front of the package and the percent total fat, which comes from the nutritional information panel. When reading the nutritional information panel make sure you are reading the value from the column that has amount per 100g of product as this will give you the percentage.

% sugar = 100% - % cocoa solids

% cocoa liquor = 2 x (% cocoa solids - % total fat)

% cocoa butter = % cocoa solids - % cocoa liquor

Example:

So substituting in for % cocoa solids:

% sugar = 100% - % cocoa solids

% sugar = 100% - 75%

% sugar = 25%

Calculating cocoa liquor content:

% cocoa liquor = 2 x (% cocoa solids - % total fat)

% cocoa liquor = 2 x (75% – 46%)

% cocoa liquor = 2 x 29%

% cocoa liquor = 58%

Calculating cocoa butter content:

% cocoa butter = % cocoa solids - % cocoa liquor

% cocoa butter = 75% - 58%

% cocoa butter = 17%

So the chocolate formulation is:

58% cocoa liquor
17% cocoa butter
25% sugar

Milk Chocolate Calculator

This is a bit more complicated than a dark chocolate, so you will need the percent cocoa solids, the percent total fat and the percent total sugars from the chocolate package.

% milk powder = (100% - % cocoa solids - % total sugars) / 0.64

% sugar = 100% - % cocoa solids - % milk powder

% cocoa butter = 2[% total fat – (0.26 x % milk powder) – (0.5 x % cocoa solids)]

% cocoa liquor = % cocoa solids - % cocoa butter

Example:

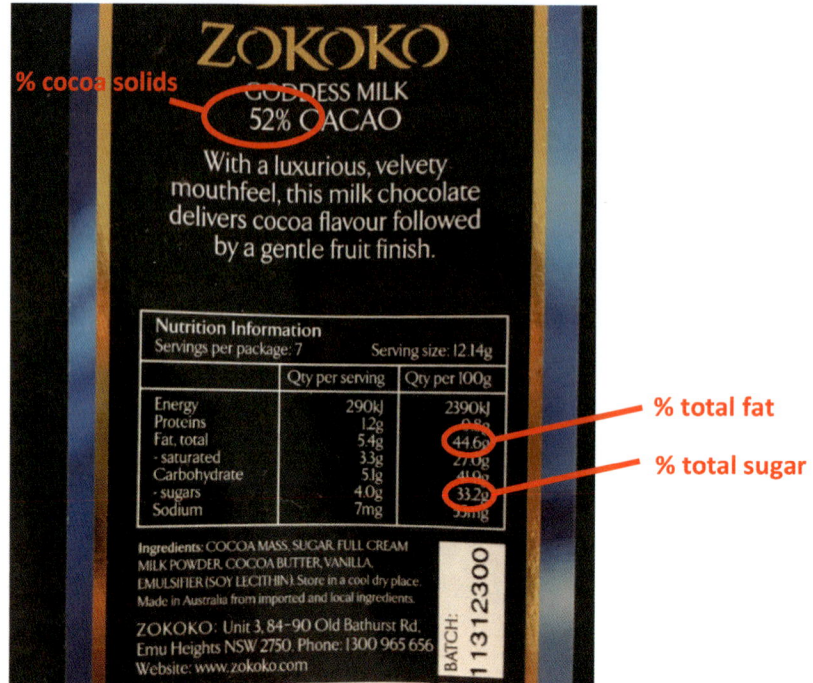

So substituting in for % cocoa solids and % total sugars

% milk powder = (100% - % cocoa solids - % total sugars) / 0.64

% milk powder = (100% – 52% - 33.2%) / 0.64

% milk powder = 14.8% / 0.64

% milk powder = 23.1%

Calculating sugar content:

% sugar = 100% - % cocoa solids - % milk powder

% sugar = 100% - 52% - 23.1%

% sugar = 24.9%

Calculating cocoa butter content:

% cocoa butter = 2[% total fat – (0.26 x % milk powder) – (0.5 x % cocoa solids)]

% cocoa butter = 2[44.6% - (0.26 x 23.1%) – (0.5 x 52%)]

% cocoa butter = 2[44.6% - 6.006% - 26%]

% cocoa butter = 2 x 12.594

% cocoa butter = 25.2%

Calculating cocoa liquor content:

% cocoa liquor = % cocoa solids - % cocoa butter

% cocoa liquor = 52% - 25.2%

% cocoa liquor = 26.8%

So the chocolate formulation is:

Milk powder 23.1%
Sugar 24.2%
Cocoa butter 25.2%
Cocoa liquor 26.8%

This is a total of 99.3% which is a result of the error in the data taken from the packaging and the approximations I am using for the fat content of cocoa beans, milk powder etc. I am also not accounting for very minor ingredients such as vanilla and lethicin. However, this method of deconstructing chocolate will get you pretty close to the actual formulation, close enough for you to start experimenting. If you wanted to formulate your chocolate with what has been calculated above, just adjust some of the percentages a little to make it up to 100%. For example increasing the cocoa liquor to 27% and milk powder to 23.6% will give a total of 100% in the above formulation.

Adding Ingredients to the Grinder

Do this in the same way as previously described. The additional ingredient of cocoa butter should be melted before adding to the mixture in the grinder. This can be easily done in a Pyrex jug in the microwave for a couple of minutes. This is easier than melting cocoa liquor as there is little chance of burning cocoa butter; still, only a few minutes will be necessary.

Dark Chocolate

Dark chocolate has a lot of flexibility around formulation depending on what your personal preference is and the origin of your bean. This is because of the high cocoa butter content coming from the cocoa beans but also from the extra cocoa butter you add. There are therefore no issues with small changes to these formulations as there will still be ample cocoa butter in the formulation to ensure a great temper.

100% Eating Chocolate Formulation

Cocoa butter is added in this formulation to reduce the intensity of the cocoa liquor and make it more palatable whilst still maintaining a 100% chocolate status. Conching is extremely important for this type of chocolate since the cocoa bean is the only contributor to the flavor profile unless you are using a natural cocoa butter that has not been deodorized and vanilla, of course. This is a typical commercial recipe, you can add 10% cocoa butter or only 5%, it is up to you and the intensity of the chocolate you are creating.

85% cocoa liquor
15% cocoa butter
8 mm vanilla bean/ kg of chocolate (optional)

80% Formulation

This is a formulation for those who like their chocolate intense. Again this formula can be changed to suit your taste and is extremely flexible since you have plenty of cocoa butter in the formulation to give a great temper. For example you can use 15% cocoa butter and reduce the cocoa liquor component by 5% for a milder 80% chocolate. Go and experiment.

70% cocoa liquor
10% cocoa butter
20% raw sugar
8 mm vanilla bean/ kg of chocolate (optional)

Dark Roast Formulation (75%)

I like this formulation for a darker or heavier roasted cocoa bean. It still contains the same amount of cocoa liquor as the 70% formulation below but less sugar which allows the cocoa flavor to come through more intensely and really pronounce the toasty cocoa notes.

60% cocoa liquor
15% cocoa butter
25% raw sugar
8 mm vanilla bean/ kg of chocolate (optional)

70% Formulation

This is a very typical formulation, it gives great mouthfeel and has a good level of sugar to let the cocoa flavor notes shine though. I use this formulation every time as the first chocolate I make from a batch of new beans, not only because it lets me explore the flavor of the cocoa with ease but it provides a benchmark from which to tweak the formulation.

60% cocoa liquor
10% cocoa butter
30% raw sugar
8 mm vanilla bean/ kg of chocolate (optional)

Dark Milk Chocolate

This is an extremely popular chocolate type, there is just enough milk in the formulations to take the edge off the bitterness and astringency of the beans but it still maintains the distinctiveness of the bean origin.

Fruity Origin Formulation

For a more fruity cocoa bean I find that a little more milk can be required to tame the acidity and to balance the chocolate. Obviously, experiment for yourself.

40% cocoa liquor
15% cocoa butter
15% full cream milk powder
30% raw sugar
8 mm vanilla bean/ kg of chocolate (optional)

Earthy / Chocolatey Origin Formulation

Using more earthy, chocolatey cocoa beans I want that intensity still there and with less acidity and fruitiness the milk in the formulation goes a bit further and it is balanced with less.

45% cocoa liquor
15% cocoa butter
10% full cream milk powder
30% raw sugar
8 mm vanilla bean/ kg of chocolate (optional)

Coconut Milk Chocolate Formulation

Coconut milk powder substituted directly in the dark milk chocolate formulations above is delicious especially with a fruity origin chocolate. Add to this ginger pieces when molding and you have a fantastic flavor combination.

Salted Caramel Chocolate Formulation

Just substitute the raw sugar for coconut blossom sugar and add 0.5g of sea salt for every kg of chocolate being made. This is such a moreish chocolate, put nibs in it and you will not be able to stop eating once you break into a bar.

Liquorice Chocolate Formulation

To create a beautiful liquorice chocolate use 0.75g of star anise and 0.75g of aniseed per kg of chocolate you are making. For a bit of theatre try sprinkling some black sea salt on the back of each bar…..soooooo gooooood.

Queen of Spice Chocolate Formulation

Cardamom and chocolate go brilliantly together, the Queen of Spices blended seamlessly with the Food of the Gods. Just add 1.5g of cardamom for every kg of chocolate being made.

Mocha Formulation

I encourage you to make this with a fruity cocoa bean, coffee goes so unbelievably well with a fruity cocoa! This is my most raved about chocolate.

39.2% cocoa liquor
14.7% cocoa butter
14.7% full cream milk powder
29.5% raw sugar
1.9% roasted coffee beans
8 mm vanilla bean/ kg of chocolate (optional)

Cinnamon Mocha Formulation

To create a Cinnamon Mocha chocolate just add an additional 1.5g of cinnamon per kg of chocolate into the formulation above.

Milk Chocolate

This is the type of chocolate that I had the most difficulty in creating a formulation that I like, I think this is because the amount of cocoa beans in the formulation approaches a point where distinctiveness of the bean is lost. It took me a little while but I am really happy with this formulation where the distinctiveness of the cocoa bean is still maintained in a chocolate that is not too sweet and has a good temper. I hope you enjoy this formulation too.

25% cocoa liquor
23% cocoa butter
19% full cream milk powder
33% raw sugar
8 mm vanilla bean/ kg of chocolate (optional)

Peanut Butter Chocolate

This is also essentially a milk chocolate and it has quite a soft temper but the chocolate and peanut flavors are in harmony and if you are a fan of peanut butter and chocolate this bar is for you. The universe compelled me to formulate this.

33% cocoa liquor
14.4% roasted peanuts
9.5% cocoa butter
14.3% full cream milk powder
28.5% raw sugar
0.5g sea salt / kg or chocolate
8 mm vanilla bean/ kg of chocolate (optional)

REPLACING COCOA BEANS

With ever increasing amounts of cocoa butter, milk powder and sugar in today's chocolate it isn't any wonder that the cocoa beans have been removed entirely and we have white chocolate. The removal of cocoa beans from the formulation allows tremendous scope for chocolate makers to become inventive, creating an avenue to add something back in or showcase a particular element or number of elements in the confection that you create. In this section I cover the replacement of cocoa beans with nuts, coffee, fruit, carob and spices, creating a diverse group of chocolate like foods.

Tempering

The tempering of these non-cocoa bean chocolates can be slightly different in that as you heat them up to melt them at the start of the tempering process, they will initially melt and become runny but as they approach 40°C they may thicken slightly or even a lot. This is nothing to worry about. As the chocolate cools down again it will become thin and runny again and then approach the thick toothpaste consistency, as it cools further, where it is time to heat it up slightly to complete the tempering process. Refer to the tempering section on page 19.

Deconstructing Commercial White Chocolate

These deconstructions will work for white chocolates formulated with sugar, cocoa butter, full cream milk powder and skim milk powder. White chocolates containing ingredients such as lactose, whey powder, clarified butter, ghee, cream powder or nuts will not be able to be deconstructed using the following formulas.

Be aware that some ingredients will list milk powder as an ingredient without stipulating whether it is full cream or skim (as in the worked example for the Whittaker's chocolate below). Usually it is a combination and you will need to use the calculator which includes skim milk powder as a component.

Formulation calculators assume the following:

1. White chocolate is composed of sugar, cocoa butter, full cream milk powder and skim milk powder. This calculation doesn't take into account the small amount of lecithin or vanilla added to certain chocolates.
2. The calculator doesn't work if lactose, cream powder, whey powder, nuts, clarified butter or anything else that isn't stipulated above, has been used as an ingredient in the chocolate.
3. That percent cocoa solids is cocoa liquor/mass/beans + cocoa butter and since there is no cocoa liquor used in white chocolate cocoa solids = cocoa butter content.
4. That full cream milk powder contains 26% fat and 36% lactose (type of sugar).
5. That skim milk powder contains 52% lactose and no fat.

White Chocolate without Skim Milk Powder Calculator

You will need the percent cocoa solids from the packet. This is equivalent to the percent cocoa butter since no cocoa beans are used in white chocolate. The other piece of information you will need from the packet is the percent total fat which can be found in the nutritional information panel. When reading the nutritional information panel make sure you are reading the value from the column that has amount per 100g of product as this will give you the percentage.

% cocoa butter = % cocoa solids

% full milk powder = (% total fat - % cocoa butter) / 0.26

% sugar = 100% - % cocoa butter - % full milk powder

Example:

So substituting in for % cocoa solids:

% cocoa butter = % cocoa solids

% cocoa butter = 40%

Calculating full milk powder content:

% full milk powder = % total fat - % cocoa butter
                     —————————————————————————
                              0.26

% full milk powder = 47% - 40%
                     ————————
                        0.26

% full milk powder = 7%
                     ————
                     0.26

% full milk powder = 27%

Calculating sugar content:

% sugar = 100% - % cocoa butter - % full milk powder

% sugar = 100% - 40% - 27%

% sugar = 33%

So the chocolate formulation is:

40% cocoa butter
27% full milk powder
33% sugar

White Chocolate with Skim Milk Powder Calculator

You will additionally need the percent total sugar information from the package.

% cocoa butter = % cocoa solids

% full milk powder = % total fat - % cocoa butter
                     —————————————————————————
                              0.26

% skim milk powder = 100% - % total sugar - % cocoa solids – (0.64 x % full milk powder)
                     ——
                                                0.48

% sugar = 100% - % cocoa butter - % full milk powder - % skim milk powder

Example:

So substituting for percent cocoa solids:

% cocoa butter = % cocoa solids

% cocoa butter = 28%

Calculating full milk powder content:

% full milk powder = (% total fat - % cocoa butter) / 0.26

% full milk powder = (31.4% - 28%) / 0.26

% full milk powder = 3.4 / 0.26

% full milk powder = 13%

Calculating skim milk powder content:

% skim milk powder = (100% - % total sugar - % cocoa solids – (0.64 x % full milk powder)) / 0.48

% skim milk powder = (100% - 56% - 28% – (0.64 x 13%)) / 0.48

% skim milk powder = 16% - 8.32%
                         0.48

% skim milk powder = 7.68
                     0.48

% skim milk powder = 16%

Calculating the sugar content:

% sugar = 100% - % cocoa butter - % full milk powder - % skim milk powder

% sugar = 100% - 28% - 13% - 16%

% sugar = 43%

So the chocolate formulation is:

28% cocoa butter
13% full milk powder
16% skim milk powder
43% sugar

This calculation will only be an estimation which is a result of the error in the data taken from the packaging and the approximations I am using for the fat and sugar content of milk powder. I am also not accounting for very minor ingredients such as vanilla and lethicin. However, this method of deconstructing chocolate will get you pretty close to the actual formulation, close enough for you to start experimenting. You can check the calculations in this case back against the packaging which stipulates that there should be 30% milk powder content and if you add the percentages calculated for full milk powder and skim milk powder you get 29%, which is pretty good.

White Chocolate

I think of white chocolate as a vehicle to showcase any number of the typical ingredients in white chocolate. You may have access to a certain type of milk powder or gourmet sugar you wish to showcase or you may have

access to a really beautiful single origin cocoa butter or you might be making your own cocoa butter. For me, I love vanilla and I take exception to the term vanilla being used as a synonym for the mundane. Vanilla is a wonderful and complex food with its own varietals and *terroir* influenced flavor profiles. Try *Vanilla tahitensis* vs *Vanilla planifolia* in the following recipe to experience the differences in vanilla. Both types of vanilla are usually readily available.

40% cocoa butter
32% raw sugar
28% full cream milk powder
20 mm vanilla bean per kg of chocolate being made

Nut Chocolate

Skim milk powder comes into its own in nut chocolates since nuts contain a significant amount of unsaturated fat which makes it more difficult to get a crisp temper in the chocolate. Skim milk powder has virtually no fat where as full milk powder has about 25% fat. Essentially what we are doing here is adding the fat back to skim milk powder as nut fat.

This formulation works for nuts which have a fat content around 60% or less; I have made suggestions in the formula. For almonds you can leave the skin on as they add distinctive almond flavor and provide a gorgeous color to the chocolate.

For the best results roast your nuts just prior to using them.

35% cocoa butter
30% raw sugar
20% skim milk powder
15% roasted peanuts, almonds or hazelnuts
0.5g sea salt per kg of chocolate being made
20 mm vanilla bean per kg of chocolate being made (optional)

Go ahead and add inclusions. I like preserved ginger in the almond chocolate. Get creative with spices ground into the formulation like cinnamon or cardamom.

Coffee Chocolate

Similar to carob chocolate, coffee is quite fibrous, however coffee has a significantly stronger flavor than carob so it is easy to formulate a very strong coffee chocolate without getting to the point where the mouthfeel is adversely affected.

Espresso and DSL formulations are perfect to explore single origin coffees. I could see this type of chocolate becoming as popular as chocolate made from cocoa beans, with endless applications in cooking, coatings and for incorporation of inclusions. This stuff is delicious!

Some companies have already tried to give this stuff a commercial life but I haven't seen it take off in a very big way yet.

Latte

35.5% cocoa butter
12.5% freshly roasted coffee beans
33% raw sugar
19% full cream milk powder

Double Shot Latte

35% cocoa butter
20% freshly roasted coffee beans
30% raw sugar
15% full cream milk powder

Espresso

40% cocoa butter
30% freshly roasted coffee beans
30% raw sugar

These coffee chocolates can be paired nicely with nibs, nuts, vanilla and fruit inclusions with a whole new world of flavor combinations to explore.

Freeze Dried Fruit Chocolate

Freeze dried fruit is what is used to make fruit chocolates since it has no water content, and with freeze dried fruit so readily available with a wide variety of fruits there is enormous scope to produce a unique fruit chocolate. The use of freeze dried fruit also allows you to create a naturally flavored and colored chocolate if you are into making coated chocolates or hollow molds but are not into using food dyes.

The formula below is specific for strawberries, other freeze dried fruits differ in their flavor intensities quite a bit so you may need to tweak the % fruit to get the desired intensity. If you increase or decrease the % freeze dried fruit, correspondingly decrease or increase the % raw sugar so that the total ingredients add up to 100%.

40% cocoa butter
6% freeze dried strawberries
24% raw sugar
30% full cream milk powder
20 mm vanilla bean per kg of chocolate being made

Carob Chocolate

The wonderful thing about carob, I think, is that it requires no sweetener when formulating it into a chocolate. Carob pods or natures muesli bars contain a lot of sugar and fiber. The whole formulation comes together perfectly, which is very satisfying. The formula for carob chocolate below is for a milk chocolate as it is very difficult to formulate chocolates with higher percentages of carob because the properties of carob are very different from cacao. If a high percentage of carob is used, the chocolate becomes very cloying on the palate and does not have a nice mouth feel. Indeed carob chocolate is still a bit cloying on the palate, but that is just the way of it I am afraid.

Carob powder can be found in two types, roasted or raw. I personally like the toastiness of the roasted carob powder, however the raw powder has its place too depending on your taste. There are now some very high quality carob powders around that you can use, so don't be put off by the carob chocolate of old, take this opportunity to reinvent carob chocolate.

38% cocoa butter
24% roasted carob powder
21% full cream milk powder
17% skim milk powder
20 mm vanilla bean per kg of chocolate being made

The use of skim milk powder here just reduces the overall fat content of the formulation, if all full cream milk powder is used it is impossible to temper.

I recommend adding mint oil (8 drops per kg of chocolate) to the carob chocolate or toasted shredded coconut or almonds (10% by weight), these are all delicious. The carob flavor reminds me a bit of molasses. I think adding some cinnamon and ginger to it may make a nice gingerbread flavored carob chocolate, which would be interesting. Something for me to try.

Combination Chocolates

This is where you can be endlessly creative with the enormous number of fruits that can be freeze dried in combination with the numerous nuts and spices available. You can let your imagination run wild, how about a strawberry and almond or mango and macadamia nut chocolate or even strawberry and carob? Well yes, here they are!

Mango and Macadamia Nut

35% cocoa butter
7% freeze dried mango
28% raw sugar
20% skim milk powder
10% roasted macadamia nuts
20 mm vanilla bean per kg of chocolate being made

Strawberry and Almond

35% cocoa butter
7% freeze dried strawberries
25% raw sugar
18% skim milk powder
15% roasted almonds
20 mm vanilla bean per kg of chocolate being made

Strawberry and Carob

Again no sugar required for this as the natural sugars from the carob, strawberries and milk powder provide just enough for delicious, indulgent chocolate. Another very satisfying formulation.

38% cocoa butter
6% freeze dried strawberries
18% roasted carob powder
21% full cream milk powder
17% skim milk powder
20 mm vanilla bean per kg of chocolate being made

Layered Chocolates

Layering the different types of chocolates can create some delicious flavor combinations; the following are some that I can recommend.

Chocolate Strawberry Bar

Fill half your mold with tempered strawberry chocolate and let it set, then fill the rest of the mold with tempered dark milk chocolate. I love this stuff!

Cappuccino Bar

To make a cappuccino bar, dust your chocolate mold with a little cocoa powder then half fill with tempered white chocolate and let it set. Fill the rest of the mold with some tempered Double Shot Latte coffee chocolate. If you want you can also just dust the chocolate with cocoa powder after the molding process, as shown in the picture.

Mocha Bar

To make a mocha bar fill half your mold with tempered dark milk chocolate and let it set, then fill the rest up with tempered Espresso coffee chocolate. This chocolate will give you a powerfully flavored mouthful.

Cooking application

One of the neat things you can do with these non-cocoa bean chocolates is to cook with them like you would cook with chocolate that you buy from the shops. This gives you the opportunity to create uniquely flavored things that you would otherwise only have flavored with chocolate. This is distinct from the following Chapter, Cooking with Real Chocolate. These recipes are just some examples that I have tried that have turned out particularly well.

Strawberry Blondie

The strawberry flavor comes through beautifully in this blondie, such a nice changeup to the delicious brownie!

Ingredients

2 eggs
220g sugar
50g canola oil
50g butter melted
150g strawberry chocolate
170g plain flour
125g frozen strawberries, quartered

Method

1. Pre heat oven to 180°C.
2. Whisk the eggs and sugar together in a bowl.
3. Melt the strawberry chocolate, oil and butter in a separate bowl.
4. Combine the two mixtures well.
5. Fold in the flour.
6. Fold in the frozen strawberries.
7. Pour the mixture into a 26 X 17 cm rectangular tin lined with baking parchment.
8. Bake the Strawberry Blondie for 30 minutes at 180°C.

Midnight Slice

Cooking with the coffee chocolate opens up a whole new way to cook with coffee as it allows the user to cook with coffee without the need for water, which is incompatible with a great many dishes. Most recipes that use coffee require water to extract and transfer the coffee flavor to the dish being created and if instant coffee is used the coffee flavor is bland and generic. For example; soufflés, mousses, ganaches, fudges, as well as certain cakes, slices and biscuits are incompatible with water. However with coffee chocolate you can now simply use coffee as you would use chocolate to make the most delicious desserts with an intense, quality coffee flavor. This example recipe below is again another brownie recipe which I find is a good vehicle to test these new chocolates in.

Ingredients	Method
3eggs 300g sugar 60g canola oil 60g butter melted 150g Espresso coffee chocolate 140g plain flour	1. Pre heat oven to 180°C. 2. Whisk the eggs and sugar together in a bowl. 3. Melt the Espresso coffee chocolate, oil and butter in a separate bowl. 4. Combine the two mixtures well. 5. Fold in the flour. 6. Pour the mixture into a 26 X 17 cm rectangular tin lined with baking parchment. 7. Bake the Midnight Slice for 20-25 minutes at 180°C.

Vanilla Ice-cream / Espresso Ice-cream

I love ice-cream, but it has to be good, I have made a few ice cream recipes but I have found them icy and lacking in body. The secret, I have discovered is cocoa butter, the cocoa butter in chocolate gives ice cream awesome body and creamy texture. This ice cream recipe is so good. I have used white chocolate here but you can also use Espresso coffee chocolate in this recipe. If you want to make proper chocolate ice cream use the recipe in the following chapter, which uses cocoa liquor.

Ingredients	Method
500ml skim milk (1.5% fat content) 200g white chocolate 200g sugar ½ vanilla bean 4 egg yolks 600ml cream (35% fat content)	1. Heat 350 ml of the milk in microwave (or stove top) to 80-90°C with the split vanilla bean. Once to temperature remove the vanilla bean and pour the milk onto the roughly chopped chocolate and sugar and blend with an immersion blender. 2. Once fully incorporated transfer to a sauce pan and begin heating over low heat. 3. Add the egg yolks to the remaining cold milk and blend with an immersion blender until frothy. 4. Add the egg / milk mix to the heating chocolate slowly and whisk together. 5. Bring the mixture just to the boil and then allow to cool, transferring it into an air tight container and chill the custard in the fridge. 6. Once cold combine the chocolate custard with the cream and transfer to an ice-cream machine to churn. 7. If you don't have an ice-cream machine you can partially freeze the mixture then transfer to a blender and blend, to break up the big ice crystals. Then put back in the freezer. You can repeat this process several times until you get the texture you are after.

COOKING WITH REAL CHOCOLATE

I rarely use finished chocolate for cooking. if I do it is usually as an inclusion such as in chocolate chip cookies, otherwise I use cocoa liquor for cooking. There are very few recipes out there for using cocoa liquor or 'baking chocolate' as it is sometimes referred to. I have therefore included a number of recipes here for using cocoa liquor to make typical things that you would want to make with your own home made chocolate.

So why use cocoa liquor instead of eating chocolate? Well, firstly it will save you time and money. Why extend your grind time by adding sugar and why add expensive cocoa butter when it will just dilute the chocolate flavor? Secondly, you are most likely adding sugar to your recipe anyway so why refine it? Thirdly, cocoa liquor also gives you great control over the sweetener you use, whether it be organic, ethically traded, GM free or artificial; the decision lies with you. Finally, and most importantly, it is the amazing intensity of the chocolate flavor and the control that you have over your cooking creation. The intensity of chocolate flavor comes from the fact that cocoa liquor takes very little time to grind down to 15 microns. Extra grinding time/conching required for fine eating chocolate drives off many of the aroma compounds in the chocolate. Cooking, however, achieves this through heat, so if you started with eating chocolate you would be starting with a more aromatically depleted product and then further removing precious flavor and aroma by cooking it.

Using cocoa liquor also means that the recipes are highly accurate as cocoa beans don't vary much in terms of fat content. However, when a recipe says use dark chocolate this could mean anything from a 50% to an 85%, eating chocolate or coverture. These vary greatly in sugar content and fat content so outcomes to recipes will be variable.

So please try these recipes and enjoy the intensity that cocoa liquor will bring to your favorite desserts!

Hot Chocolates

Hot chocolates are my absolute favorite, in fact striving to make the perfect hot chocolate was one of the reasons this book exists at all. The first thing I made with cocoa liquor was a hot chocolate and it blew me away. The reason I tried it was because I liked hot chocolates but couldn't bear the ones you get at cafés, they were either too weak or too decadent or made from chocolate syrup used for milkshakes! How can chocolate be too decadent? Well, it can I can assure you. The hot chocolates I am thinking of, made from coverture and topped with cream, were greasy and awful. I tried making my own using cocoa powder, sugar and hot milk but I knew there had to be something more. Chocolate can be so intense and beautiful as something to eat, why wasn't it so with hot chocolates? Well the answer was quite simply go back to basics, roasted cocoa beans minimally refined into cocoa liquor; that is all you need!

My Ideal Hot Chocolate

   20g cocoa liquor
   15g sugar or equivalent sweetener
   240ml skim milk

The milk used for hot chocolates is skim milk with a fat content at about 1.5% which is, according to extensive tasting, the optimum for hot chocolates. Full cream milk has a higher fat content which I feel mutes the flavor of the chocolate slightly. Feel free to experiment though.

Heat the milk to about 80-90°C, this can be done easily in the microwave or on the stove. Once the milk is hot pour it onto the combined cocoa liquor and sugar/sweetener in a tall jug and blend with an immersion blender. A few pulses is enough and the hot chocolate develops a dense foam head, which is due to the cocoa butter. Pour it back into a warmed mug and enjoy. If your jug is metal or you are pouring it into a cold mug you may need to warm it again in the microwave as it will lose heat in the transfers. This hot chocolate is intense and satisfying but it is also light, not heavy and horrible like some commercial offerings.

Hot Chocolate Anatomy

In the Mayan language spoken in Yucatan, the term 'yom cacao' refers to 'chocolate foam'. I am here, now, hijacking the term 'yom' to describe the dense foam that arises when you make hot chocolates from cacao liquor and whip them thoroughly. This foam is caused by the emulsification of fats in the chocolate; the same thing occurs when an espresso is pulled and is called the crema.

Hot Chocolate and Cheese

In Columbia it is as common as spreading your bread with butter to dip cheese into a hot chocolate. The favored cheese is Quesito Casero, a soft mozzarella type of cheese. After trying many cheeses with hot chocolate I have found that mozzarella and haloumi pair well with a hot chocolate.

Affogato

This is usually a shot of espresso coffee poured over ice-cream. Sick of pouring more sugar over already sugar filled ice cream, try this for a hit, still lots of sugar but not as much as in chocolate syrup.

   30 ml (1 shot) boiling water
   7.5 g cocoa liquor
   5g sugar

Pour boiling water over the cocoa liquor and sugar and blend with an immersion blender, quickly pour over two scoops of ice-cream in a tall glass and enjoy.

cH$_2$Ocolate Drinks

A ganache does not necessarily have to be made using cream, you can use any liquid you like such as fruit juice, tea, coffee or any other water based liquid you can think of. Discovering water ganaches led me to a gold mine of possibilities for cocoa liquor! Chocolate hydrate or 'cH$_2$Ocolate', is a simple ganache comprised of cocoa liquor and water.

cH$_2$Ocolate

    200g cocoa liquor
    150ml water at 70°C

Chop or grate 200g of cocoa liquor and place in a blending jug, then add 150ml of boiled water, cooled to 70°C. Let this mixture sit for 5 minutes for the chocolate to warm through, then blend to give a glossy ganache. Transfer this to a container, put a lid on it and put it in the fridge until cold.

cH$_2$Ocolate can be stored in the fridge for about a month or so, it may gradually grow crystals of cocoa butter on it, which look like little cream colored balls. This is nothing to worry about. cH$_2$Ocolate has a high water activity so it may start to grow mold on it after a while. Mold is quite distinctive from the cocoa butter crystals. Just make sure you keep an eye on it and don't make too much at once so it is used within that month timeframe.

Once you have your cH$_2$Ocolate cold you can use it to make cold chocolate drinks using real chocolate which are ready to drink straight away. This removes the biggest challenge in making cold drinks with real chocolate, which is the need to heat some component of it to melt and incorporate the chocolate. The cold cH$_2$Ocolate makes sure that the fats are already emulsified at low temperature so just blend in cH$_2$Ocolate without a worry.

Frappé

Legend has it that 'Frappé coffee' the foamy instant coffee drink poured over crushed ice was invented by Dimitris Vakondios back in 1957 at the International Trade Fair in Thessaloniki. The Nestlé employee required his instant coffee fix but couldn't get it because he didn't have access to hot water. So serendipity prevailed and he mixed cold water, sugar and instant coffee in a Nestlé shaker that was being exhibited and on shaking produced a foamy coffee drink that became the Frappé. Here is the chocolate version!

    20g cH$_2$Ocolate
    20g sugar
    125ml milk (skim 1.5% fat)
    125g ice

Place all ingredients into a blender in the order in the ingredients list and blend until ice is finely crushed.

Chocolate Milkshake

    20g cH$_2$Ocolate
    15g powdered sugar
    250g milk (skim 1.5% fat)

Combine all ingredients in a blender jug and blend with an immersion blender, pour into a tall glass and you have the perfect creamy chocolate milkshake. Once again there is the option here to use an artificial sweetener.

Chocolate, Banana and Honey Milkshake

   1 medium banana
   1 tsp honey (or more to taste)
   20g cH$_2$Ocolate
   250ml skim milk (skim 1.5% fat)

Put all ingredients in a jug and blend with an immersion blender. Yummy!

Chocolate Fruit Smoothies

What is good about this smoothie, other than the fact that it tastes great, is that it takes advantage of the natural sugars in the fruit which is enough to sweeten the unsweetened cH$_2$Ocolate perfectly!

   1 medium banana
   125 ml pineapple juice
   125 ml apricot nectar
   15g cH$_2$Ocolate

Put all ingredients in a jug and blend with an immersion blender. Delicious!

Ganache Truffles

This recipe gives an intense chocolate truffle that is easy to mold into balls out of the fridge and gives a gloriously, luxuriantly textured truffle at room temperature (around 20-25°C). If you know it is going to be hotter, serve the truffles out of the fridge or dip them in chocolate.

Ingredients	*Method*
200ml cream (35% fat content) 120g caster sugar 180g cocoa liquor	1. Bring cream to 80°C in a sauce pan (DO NOT BOIL) 2. Add the sugar to the hot cream and stir until mostly dissolved then transfer into an immersion blender jug containing the chopped cocoa liquor. 3. Allow the mixture to sit for 5 minutes then blend with an immersion blender. 4. Allow to cool to room temperature in a container without lid on then put the lid on and refrigerate. 5. Once cold, roll into truffles and dust in cocoa powder or temper some chocolate and dip and dust. 6. If dusting the uncoated ganache, do this just before serving as the moisture from the ganache will slowly moisten the cocoa powder dusting and it will no longer be dusty.

If your ganache does split try adding a teaspoon of cold skim milk to the mixture and blending again.

Salted Chocolate Caramel Sauce

I love salted caramel and wanted to make sauce with a hint of chocolate to get a bit more umami in the mix. This sauce is the bomb, pour it over everything, ice-cream, roasted pineapple, slice of cake, banana split, whatever!

Ingredients

200g raw sugar
150g salted butter
175g cream (35% fat content)
35g cocoa liquor

Method

1. Bring sugar and butter to the boil and boil for 5 minutes constantly whisking.
2. Turn off the heat and pour in the cream all at once, whisking vigorously so as not to form lumps of caramel – be careful as it will boil vigorously.
3. If you end up with lumps of solid sugar in it just strain it through a wire mesh sieve. Do this before adding the chocolate while the caramel is still hot.
4. The last step is to add the chocolate and stir until melted and combined.

Chocolate Custard

I love chocolate custard, experience an incredible intensity of chocolate with this chocolate custard recipe.

Ingredients

250ml full cream milk
250ml cream (35% fat content)
80g sugar
4 egg yolks
25g corn flour
40g cocoa liquor

Method

1. Bring the cream and milk to 80°C.
2. Combine egg yolks, corn flour and sugar in a bowl.
3. Pour hot milk / cream mixture into the egg yolk mixture slowly with rapid whisking.
4. Once all added pour mixture back into sauce pan and heat with whisking until thick (do not boil – thickening happens at 80°C).
5. Once custard cools to about 60°C add in the cocoa liquor and stir until melted and combined.

This is not a pouring custard, it is more for layers in trifles or adding nibs too and eating cold or hot!

Avocado Chocolate Mousse

Ingredients

2 avocados
85ml skim milk
120g powdered sugar
140g cocoa liquor

Method

1. Blend avocado, milk and powdered sugar until smooth and creamy.
2. Melt the cocoa liquor and blend with the avocado mixture.
3. Served topped with chopped mixed nuts and a tiny drizzle of honey.

Serves 4-5

Chocolate Ice-cream

This is a fantastically rich chocolate ice-cream, one that you will be able to taste the distinct origin of the cocoa beans in. It is interesting to use different origins to make the ice-cream and compare them.

Ingredients	Method
120g cocoa liquor 300g sugar 500ml skim milk (1.5% fat content) 4 egg yolks 600ml cream (35% fat content)	1. Heat 350 ml of the milk in microwave (or stove top) to 80-90°C and pour onto the cocoa liquor and sugar and blend with an immersion blender. 2. Once fully incorporated transfer to a sauce pan and begin heating over low heat. 3. Add the egg yolks to the remaining cold milk and blend with an immersion blender until frothy. 4. Add the egg / milk mix to the heating chocolate slowly and whisk together. 5. Bring the mixture just to the boil and then allow to cool, transferring it into an air tight container and chill the custard in the fridge. 6. Once cold combine the chocolate custard with the cream and transfer to an ice-cream machine to churn. 7. If you don't have an ice-cream machine you can partially freeze the mixture then transfer to a blender and blend, to break up the big ice crystals. Then put back in the freezer. You can repeat this process several times until you get the texture you are after.

Rice Pudding

I love rice pudding, so a chocolate version was inevitable.

Ingredients	Method
70g Arborio rice 450ml full cream milk 40g caster sugar 30g cocoa liquor	1. Wash rice thoroughly about 6 times with water and drain. 2. Place the rice in a saucepan and add the cold milk and heat until boiling, simmer until rice is tender and the milk reduced. 3. I usually simmer for about 20 minutes and then turn the heat off and put the saucepan lid on and let sit for 10 min. 4. Once the rice is cooked add the caster sugar and stir in until dissolved then add the cocoa liquor and stir until combined. 5. Serve immediately or divide amongst 2 ramekins and refrigerate. 6. Again I love it cold or hot with cocoa nibs stirred through.

Chocolate Fissure Cookies

These are delicious cookies and showcase the origin of the chocolate very well. You will not be able to stop at just one. My daughters love making and eating these cookies!

Ingredients

140-160g plain flour
1 tsp baking powder
Pinch of salt
230g sugar
2 eggs
100g cocoa liquor melted
Powdered sugar (for dusting)

Method

1. Pre-heat oven to 180°C.
2. Combine the flour (140g), salt and baking powder and set aside.
3. Beat eggs and sugar and then add melted cocoa liquor, beating quickly so as not to set the cocoa liquor.
4. Combine the dry ingredients with the chocolate mixture and knead into a sticky dough.
5. You may need to adjust the mixture with the extra flour, so it starts to hold together (stickiness seems to depend on the size of the eggs).
6. Wrap the dough in plastic wrap and refrigerate for at least a couple of hours.
7. Make the dough into balls and slightly flatten, heavily dust with powdered sugar and place on a well-greased baking tray.
8. Bake for 15 minutes, be careful as the bottoms can burn easily due to the icing sugar coating.

Makes about 30 cookies.

Chocolate Brownie

Chocolate brownies are my absolute favorite. Delicious on their own but you can take them to the next level with cream, ice-cream and a delicious dessert sauce.

Ingredients	*Method*
3 eggs 325g sugar 60g canola oil 60g butter 150g cocoa liquor 140g plain flour	1. Pre heat oven to 180°C. 2. Whisk the eggs and sugar together in a bowl, melt the cocoa liquor, oil and butter in a separate bowl. 3. Combine the two mixtures and then fold in the flour. 4. Pour the mixture into a 26 X 17 cm rectangular tin lined with baking parchment. 5. Bake the brownie for 20 minutes. 6. The brownie is cooked when the edges are done and the middle has just formed the nice shiny flaky surface.

Adding berries or nuts is a great addition to the chocolate brownie, around about 100-125g of any fruit or nut will work well in this recipe.

Chocolate Soufflé

Soufflés are wonderful but you have to be prepared and work quickly to be successful!

Ingredients	*Method*
100g cocoa liquor melted 100g caster sugar 5 egg yolks 7 egg whites	1. Pre-heat the oven to 200°C. 2. Butter 5 x 250ml ramekins and dust the inside with caster sugar – just put a spoonful of the sugar in and pour it out twisting so that it sticks to all inside surfaces. 3. Whip the egg whites to stiff peaks. 4. Whisk the room temperature egg yolks with the sugar and then add the melted cocoa liquor stirring vigorously, to this add ¼ of the egg whites and beat in. This must be done quickly as the chocolate, sugar egg mixture will set hard. 5. Once you have a smooth fluffy batter gently fold in the remaining beaten egg whites until just combined. 6. Fill ramekins to the brim then run your thumb around the edge of the batter to make an edge so the soufflé rises properly.

Baked Chocolate Cheesecake

I love a good baked chocolate cheesecake but I really hate cheese cake bases. This recipe is incredible, I got the recipe right the first time and to rave reviews from the poor folks who were forced to taste it. I wanted to create a base that would be at the same level as the filling in terms of scrumptiousness and I think I have achieved that.

Ingredients

Base
50g wafer
100g almond meal
50g caster sugar
70g cocoa liquor
60g butter

Filling
500g cream cheese
250g sour cream
4 eggs
200g caster sugar
25g corn flour
200g cocoa liquor melted

Method

Base
1. Pre-heat oven to 150°C.
2. Combine the wafer, almond meal and caster sugar in a blender and blend to a crumb.
3. Melt the butter and cocoa liquor together.
4. Stir the crumb into the butter / cocoa liquor mixture.
5. Press the base crumb into the baking paper lined base of a 9 inch round spring-form pan and chill for 15 min in the fridge.
6. Bake the base at 150°C for 20 minutes and remove to cool to room temperature.

Filling
7. Combine the cream cheese and sour cream using a stand mixer.
8. Add eggs one at a time, beating well between additions.
9. Mix the caster sugar and corn flour together well and then add to the mixture in the stand mixer and combine.
10. Lastly add the melted cocoa liquor and mix well.
11. Once the baked base is cool pour in the filling (keep back anything that doesn't fit) and bake for 1 hour and 10 min at 150°C. The middle should still be a little bit wobbly.

Chocolate Truffle Tart

Truffle tarts are a great way to impress and feed a lot of people for dessert, since they are so rich all you need is a thin slice……apparently.

Ingredients

Chocolate Pastry
100g butter
45g dark brown sugar
75g cocoa liquor
200g plain flour
1 egg yolk
30ml chilled water

Caramelized Nibs
120g caster sugar
1 cup cocoa nibs

Ganache
200ml cream (35% fat content)
120g caster sugar
180g cocoa liquor

Method

Chocolate Pastry
1. Blitz butter and dark brown sugar in a food processor until combined.
2. Add melted cocoa liquor and blend until a smooth paste.
3. Quickly add the flour in three portions and blitz until you have an even crumb.
4. Transfer the pastry crumb to a mixing bowl.
5. Add egg yolk and mix in the water and bring pastry together, do not over work.
6. Wrap in glad wrap and refrigerate for a minimum 30 min.
7. Roll out to fit a 27.5 cm tart case with removable base.
8. Prick base all over with a fork, trim the edges, refrigerate case while pre-heating oven to 200°C.
9. Cook the base at this temperature for 15 minutes.
10. Remove from oven and cool completely to room temp.

Caramelized Nibs

11. Heat sugar in a saucepan slowly until melted and a light caramel color.
12. Add nibs and stir rapidly until all covered and then scrape / pour out onto a baking tray to cool.
13. Break up the caramelized nibs and use half to layer the cool tart casing.

Ganache

14. Bring cream to 80°C in a sauce pan (DO NOT BOIL)
15. Add the sugar to the hot cream and stir until mostly dissolved then transfer into an immersion blender jug containing the chopped cocoa liquor.
16. Allow the mixture to sit for 5 minutes then blend with an immersion blender.
17. Pour over the caramelized nibs in the pastry casing and shake gently to get an even surface.
18. Use the remaining nibs to sprinkle over the top or store in air tight container for next time or just eat them as a snack. Refrigerate to set ganache and then serve.

The caramel will soften and melt away under the ganache and the nibs will soften over time so this tart is best eaten within a couple of hours of making for maximum crunch! Omit the caramelized nibs if you like.

INDEX

Avocado		47
Bay leaf		11
Cacao beans		
-	Broken	4
-	Clusters	3
-	Cracking	5
-	Cut	4
-	Fermentation	1-2
-	Flat	3
-	Germinated	4
-	Mini	3
-	Moldy	2
-	Roasting	4-5, 15
-	Sorting	3-4
-	Storing	2-3
-	Winnowing	5-6
Caramelized Nibs		52
Cardamom		11, 17, 30
cH$_2$Ocolate		45-46
Chocolate		
-	Affogato	44
-	Brownie	41-42, 50
-	Caramel sauce	47
-	Carob	38-40
-	Cheesecake	51
-	Coating	20
-	Coconut milk	17, 29
-	Coffee	11, 17, 19, 30, 37, 40, 42
-	Commercial style	22-27, 31-35
-	Cookies	49
-	Custard	47
-	Dark	17, 23-25, 28-29
-	Dark milk	17, 23, 25-27, 29-30
-	Frappé	45
-	Freeze Dried Fruit	18, 20, 38, 39-41
-	Hot	44
-	Ice-cream	42, 48
-	Inclusions	18, 21
-	Milk	23, 25-27, 30
-	Milkshake	45-46
-	Mocha	11, 17, 30, 41
-	Mousse	47
-	Nut	14, 18, 20-21, 30, 36, 39-40
-	Pastry	51
-	Percentage	13
-	Raw	16
-	Rice pudding	48
-	Sauce	47
-	Single origin	14
-	Spread	20-21
-	Strawberry	38, 39-40, 41
-	Soufflé	50
-	Tart	51
-	Truffles	46
-	White	31-36
Cinnamon		11, 30
Cloves		11
Cocoa butter		9-10, 22
Cocoa liquor		
-	Cooking with	43-52
-	Flavoring	10-12
-	Making	7-8
-	Depleted	9-10, 18, 21
Coconut		19, 39
Coconut blossom sugar		15, 17, 29
Coffee		11, 17, 19, 30, 37, 40, 42
Conching		9, 16
Coriander		19
Coverture		22
Creole		11
Dried fruit		18, 21
Fats and oils		13, 15
Fennel		18
Freeze dried fruit		18, 20, 38, 39-40, 41
Ganache		
-	Cream	46, 52
-	Water	45-46
Ginger		11, 17, 19
Gingerbread		11
Grinder		7
Grinding		8-9, 16, 27
Honeycomb		19, 20
Jasmine		11-12
Lethicin		22-23
Liquorice		11, 29
Malt powder		15
Midnight slice		42
Milk powder		14, 17-18, 25-27, 31-36
Mint oil		10, 39
Mocha		11, 17, 30, 41
Molding		20
Molds		20
Nibs		6, 18, 21, 52
Nuts		14, 18, 20-21, 30, 36, 39-40
Orange oil		10
Stone grinder		7-9
Strawberry blondie		41
Salt		15, 18, 19, 29
Sugar		13, 14
Tempering		10, 19-20, 31
Vanilla		11, 15, 19, 23, 42
Water		13, 45
Winnowing		5-6

Thomas D Avery

ABOUT THE AUTHOR

I remember quite clearly when I was bitten by the chocolate bug. I was sitting in my parents' apartment in Brisbane, Australia, back in May 2007 with a computer in front of me. I had just been thinking about Dad's coffee plant, growing in a pot on the balcony. The thought of growing and making your own coffee quite appealed to me but I don't drink coffee, in fact I didn't have any vices, I am not a huge fan of tea or wine or beer or anything that might be considered something to be a connoisseur of. In any case the thought struck me, could I grow cacao on the balcony and then make chocolate? At this stage I knew I loved chocolate, as almost everyone does, but I didn't know how much and I only vaguely knew about fine chocolate, where the flavor profile is as important and regarded as a fine wine. The first two websites that caught my eye were an Australian website created by a company known as Tava, to sell their 100% cacao bars (cocoa liquor) and Chocolate Alchemy, a site run by John Nanci who made chocolate from bean-to-bar on a kitchen scale. Through his site he sold beans, grinders and all the other equipment and ingredients to make chocolate and ran a forum on the making of chocolate at home. So right then and there I decided I would make chocolate too, and it was a good decision!

I proceeded to purchase a stone grinder, the same one that I still currently use and some cocoa beans to get started. I joined in the forum discussions and built winnowers and tried to express my own cocoa butter, talked about formulations and started buying chocolate from newly emerging bean-to-bar chocolate makers. I took to chocolate making with great enthusiasm and my background in synthetic chemistry gave me a sound understanding of all the processes. I was fortunate to be doing this at a time when the bean-to-bar chocolate scene was really taking off in the USA and benefited from these chocolate makers getting on online forums Chocolate Alchemy and Clay Gordon's The Chocolate Life and exchanging ideas. Along with this many cacao growers were also making use of these forums looking for customers for their single origin beans. I found an excellent way to collaborate with these growers, many of whom were interested in how their beans would translate into fine chocolate. I would receive small lots of beans from growers from around the world, roast them and turn them into chocolate and then send the chocolate back to the grower with my tasting notes. This worked out beautifully; no money was exchanged, instead the grower paid for the shipping of beans to me and I paid for the shipping of chocolate back to them. We both got to taste the chocolate and I gained a wealth of knowledge about fermentation practices and other post-harvest practices and how they impact the flavor of the finished chocolate. Not to mention extensive experience with many different cacao origins which was interesting and delicious. I was very fortunate to become involved with Don Murday a cacao grower in far north Queensland, Australia, just as the Australian growers were getting serious about cacao and chocolate production. I did a lot of work with him fine tuning fermentation practices, which was a very interesting project. The other thing that was fantastic about this was that he became a good friend; I still to this day send him bars from every batch of chocolate I make.

I felt humbled recently by an acknowledgement from Kablon Farms in the Philippines which attribute my endorsement of their beans to their success. They had fabulous beans and a fabulous committed team, all I did was give them the confidence that they had a product worthy of development.

> *It took a ringing endorsement from a certain Dr Thomas Avery from Australia to affirm Kablon Farms' belief in the world-class quality of their cacao beans. Avery, who got hold of the beans following Ernesto Pantua Jr's offer on a blog site TheChocolateLife to send the dried beans to a chosen chocolatier from anywhere in the world, called the batch "the best beans he has ever worked with", and deemed its fermentation "immaculate".*
>
> *An now, the world has Dr Avery to thank for what has led to the healthy, all natural, dark chocolate products from Kablon Farms. Their selection of chocolate products that include dark, raw and spicy chocolate bars allow for the rest of the world to bring home the best of Mindanaoan flavours.*
> - Excerpt from Philippine tourism magazine for international release: **Expat Travel & Lifestyle: Philippines, June 2017**

Chocolate making has been a wonderful hobby, one I unfortunately have not had the opportunity or circumstances to permit me to develop it commercially. This book is my way of sharing many years of research, discovery, invention, recipe and formulation development. The formulations and recipes in this book are tailored to my taste and philosophies, however, I hope I have provided the tools and knowledge for you to create fabulous chocolate in your own style. The more people making chocolate in the world the better!

ACKNOWLEDGEMENTS

I am extremely grateful for all the friends I have made in chocolate and all the growers who trusted me with their beans! Thank you to my wife Michelle and daughters Imogen and Maple for tasting and providing feedback on the chocolate and recipes in this book. Thank you to my mum Elizabeth Avery and mother-in-law Joan Lowndes for editing this book. And thank you to my neighbors Rhys Driver and Scott Tunn for helping me out with Photoshop and CreateSpace programs!

Printed in Great Britain
by Amazon